ORIGIN AND OBJECTS

OF THE

SLAVEHOLDERS' CONSPIRACY

AGAINST DEMOCRATIC PRINCIPLES,

AS WELL AS

AGAINST THE NATIONAL UNION—

ILLUSTRATED IN THE

SPEECHES OF ANDREW JACKSON HAMILTON,

IN THE STATEMENTS OF LORENZO SHERWOOD, EX-MEMBER OF THE TEXAN LEGISLATURE, AND IN THE PUBLICATIONS OF THE DEMOCRATIC LEAGUE, &c.

THE SLAVE ARISTOCRACY AGAINST DEMOCRACY.

STATEMENTS ADDRESSED TO LOYAL MEN OF ALL PARTIES,
CONCERNING THE
ANTAGONISTIC PRINCIPLES INVOLVED IN THE REBELLION—

By HENRY O'RIELLY.

NEW YORK, OCTOBER, 1862:
BAKER & GODWIN, PRINTERS,
PRINTING-HOUSE SQUARE, OPPOSITE CITY HALL.

ORIGIN AND OBJECTS

OF THE

Slaveholders' Conspiracy against Democratic Principles,

AS WELL AS AGAINST

THE NATIONAL UNION,

ILLUSTRATED IN THE

SPEECHES OF ANDREW JACKSON HAMILTON,

IN THE STATEMENTS OF LORENZO SHERWOOD, EX-MEMBER OF THE TEXAN LEGISLATURE, AND IN THE PUBLICATIONS OF THE DEMOCRATIC LEAGUE, &c.

ANTAGONISTIC PRINCIPLES INVOLVED IN THE REBELLION—THE SLAVE ARISTOCRACY against THE DEMOCRACY.

The commentaries on the recent speeches of Col. Hamilton, of Texas, by several prominent New York journalists, furnish appropriate introduction to the outlines of those speeches which are herewith presented for the consideration of loyal men of all parties throughout the land.

It will be seen that, much as they may differ in other respects, *The World & Courier & Enquirer*, the *Tribune*, the *Times*, and the *Evening Post*, concur in ranking those speeches among the most important ever made in connection with the origin and objects of the Slaveholders' Rebellion.

On some points, indeed, the revelations of Col. Hamilton are considered as the most valuable—inasmuch as they show, by the highest *Southern* testimony, the breadth, depth, and blackness of that conspiracy against the individual rights of the Democratic masses, as well as against the integrity of the National Union.

"The Northern People have accepted this war on too narrow grounds altogether," says *The World & Courier & Enquirer*:—"They have comprehended but a very meagre portion of the real interests at stake—for the very good reason that they have hardly begun to understand the spirit and aims of the Rebel leaders. Had there been a better appreciation of the actual truth, the war would never have lagged as it has been suffered to do from the beginning."

"The evidence of such men as Col. Hamilton, who is fresh from the active scenes of the Rebellion, and who has watched it with penetrating eye from its first step, is of peculiar value," says the *World* in its daily issue of the 4th of October. "Their conclusions, formed on the spot, face to face with the monster, are of infinitely more weight than the notions of Northern men, who know it only by occasional glimpses in the far distance. It is well that their testimony should be brought before our public whenever it can be obtained. The gentlemen who have induced Col. Hamilton to address our people with instruction and appeal, have done the good cause precious service." * * * "Col. Hamilton has no hesitation in pronouncing the issue now pending to be THE VERY HIGHEST, AND BROADEST, AND DEEPEST possible. It is, to his mind, nothing more nor less than A STRUGGLE BETWEEN THE ULTIMATE PRINCIPLES OF CIVIL GOVERNMENT—a question whether *the rule of the few* or *the rule of the many* shall prevail. He presents it as his settled conviction that *the leaders* in this Rebellion are actuated by a distinct purpose to SUPPLANT POPULAR GOVERNMENT and ESTABLISH A MONARCHY—and that this comes from their belief that *Slavery can have no effectual safeguard except what the strongest form of government can afford*. Therefore, he warns us not to rest upon the idea that mere territory, or even mere nationality, is at stake in this conflict."

"What has really got to be decided, as he justly views it," adds the *World*, "is, not whether the flag itself shall be deprived of a third of its stars, or whether the flag itself shall continue to exist, but *whether the Republican principle*, which has given the flag all its glory, *is or is not to perish*. He rightly declares that the co-existence of a Monarchy and a Republic between the Great Lakes and the Gulf is a civil impossibility—that such an experiment would only be *another name for perpetual war*.

"We are, therefore, shut up to the absolute necessity of meeting this question now, once for all," continues the *World*—"and, in fidelity to the great principles of the Declaration of Independence which our forefathers sealed with their blood, are bound to prosecute this war with an energy and a self-devotion far beyond anything we have yet displayed. These are great facts which Col. Hamilton seeks to enforce. He talks like a man who is thoroughly pervaded by a sense of their awful moment—and no mind that heeds his disclosures and his arguments, can doubt that he is right."

Profoundly impressed with the same views that Col. Hamilton has now forcibly illustrated by his speeches in New York and Brooklyn, the DEMOCRATIC LEAGUE FOR SUSTAINING THE NATIONAL UNITY has earnestly labored for several months in disseminating documents replete with facts and arguments on the important topics. And some of those important documents are now republished in connection with the speeches of Col. Hamilton, as showing the identity of views between the Colonel and that League—one of whose most efficient members (Lorenzo Sherwood) was a resident and a legislator in Texas, and a co-worker with Col. Hamilton in sustaining the National Government in Texas, till its flag and its forces were betrayed by the General (Twiggs) whom the then War Secretary Floyd placed in command as an emissary of Rebellion.

As the importance of the topics cannot be over-estimated, it is hoped that men of all parties will thoroughly examine these and other publications calculated to place the origin and objects of the Slaveholders' Conspiracy in their true light—as an attempted revolution not only in the Union of the States, but in the relations of the Democratic masses to the government of their country—that each man may act and vote as becomes an American citizen, in view of the fact which Col. Hamilton concurs with the Democratic League in asserting, that "the leaders in this "Rebellion are actuated by a distinct purpose to supplant popular government and establish a monarchy; and that "this comes from their belief that Slavery can have no effectual safeguard except what the strongest government "can afford;" or, as Mr. Garnett, of Virginia, in his letter to Trescott (Mr. Buchanan's Assistant Secretary of State), expresses it, when "objecting to the term Democrat," because, as slaveholders declared, "*Democracy*, in its original philosophical sense, is, indeed, *incompatible with Slavery and the whole system of Southern Society*."

NEW-YORK, OCTOBER, 1862.

HENRY O'RIELLY.

[INTRODUCTORY.]

THE SPEECHES OF COL. HAMILTON, OF TEXAS.

(From the "World and Courier and Enquirer," of Oct. 4—friendly to Seymour.)

The greatest difficulty, from the outset, in the way of a just appreciation by the North of the real nature of this rebellion, has been the fact that the loyal men who knew most of it were least able to give their testimony. The last echoes of the cannon at Sumter had hardly died away before the communications between the two sections were closed; and the northern mind was left to only casual and desultory means of learning the developments of the astounding iniquity.

The consequence was that it was very slow to apprehend the real malignity and scope of the treason. The Government and the people generally were disposed to regard it as a wild movement cunningly got up by a few restless spirits, and easily quelled. The driblets of information that came over the rebel borders were so indefinite and contradictory that they served only to confuse and mislead.

It has been by terrible experience alone that northern misjudgments have gradually been corrected — an experience that has cost the country an amount of treasure and blood dreadful to contemplate. And yet, in spite of all this, a thousand misconceptions still exist.

There is yet a widely prevailing tendency to ascribe the rebellion to mere secondary and minor causes, and to believe that it will cost only a little more effort to sweep it from the land forever.

The habit still clings of reasoning from the old data. We unconsciously base half of our judgments upon facts as they used to be, instead of facts as they are. This comes from the difficulty of correctly learning present developments.

Therefore, the evidence of such men as Col. Hamilton, who is fresh from the active scenes of the rebellion, and who has watched it with penetrating eye from its first step, is of peculiar value. Their conclusions, formed on the very spot, face to face with the monster, are of infinitely more weight than the notions of northern men who know it only by occasional glimpses in the far distance. It is well that their testimony should be brought before our public whenever it can be obtained. The gentlemen who have induced Colonel Hamilton to address our people with instruction and appeal, have done the good cause precious service. Winging their way, as these speeches do, by the press, through every loyal state, they will have a salutary influence of no small moment in the present critical period of the war.

Colonel Hamilton has no hesitation in pronouncing the issue now pending to be *the very highest*, and *broadest*, and *deepest* possible.

It is to his mind nothing more nor less than a struggle between the ultimate principles of civil Government—a question whether *the rule of the few*, or *the rule of the many*, shall prevail. He presents it as his settled conviction that the leaders in this rebellion are actuated by a distinct purpose to SUPPLANT POPULAR GOVERNMENT and establish a MONARCHY; and that this comes from their belief that *slavery can have no effectual safeguard except what the strongest form of Government can afford.* Therefore, he warns us not to rest upon the idea that mere territory, or even mere nationality, is at stake in this conflict.

What has really got to be decided, as he justly views it, is not whether the flag shall be deprived of a third of its stars, or whether the flag itself shall continue to exist, but *whether the republican principle*, which has given the flag all its glory, *is or is not to perish.* He rightly declares that the coexistence of a monarchy and a republic between the great Lakes and the Gulf is a civil impossibility—that such an experiment would only be another name for perpetual war.

We are, therefore, shut up to the absolute necessity of meeting this question now, once for all; and, in fidelity to the great principles of the Declaration of Independence which our forefathers sealed with their blood, are bound to prosecute this war with an energy and a self-devotion far beyond anything we have yet displayed.

These are great facts which Colonel Hamilton seeks to enforce. He talks like a man who is thoroughly pervaded by a sense of their awful moment; and *no mind that heeds his disclosures and his arguments can doubt that he is right.*

The Northern people have accepted this war on too narrow grounds altogether. They have comprehended but a very meagre portion of the real interests at stake; for the very good reason that they have hardly begun to understand the spirit and aims of the rebel leaders. Had there been a better appreciation of the actual truth, the war would never have lagged as it has been suffered to do from the beginning. The twenty millions of the North could never have lived for eighteen live-long months as they have done under the shadow of such a terrific danger. By an irresistible impulse they would have closed in with it forthwith, and made an end of it. Nobody doubts that they had the ability. There is no power on the continent that could for an instant stand against their collected energy. What was wanting was not the strength, but the due sense of infinite peril. Even at this late day *this feeling needs to be strengthened*, and the man who does this so intelligently and so faithfully as this Southern patriot deserves to be hailed as a public benefactor.

Listening to Col. Hamilton, the conviction comes home afresh to us that we of the North, too, need everywhere and always to preserve that eternal vigilance which is the price of liberty. It is by small beginnings that constitutional liberty is first undermined. It is under the highest and purest pretexts that the rights of citizens are first infringed upon. It is for every patriot to oppose these beginnings.

Col. HAMILTON'S First Speech in the North.

THE REBELLION AGAINST DEMOCRACY—

ITS CAUSES AND CONSEQUENCES.

NEW YORK, Oct. 1, 1862.

HON. A. J. HAMILTON.—Dear Sir: As it is understood that you are to remain in town some few days, it would be gratifying to the friends of the Union if you would consent to address an audience at the Academy of Music, in Brooklyn, on Thursday evening, the 2d of October inst., on the subject of the rebellion. We know of no one who could better elucidate the motives and reasonings that led the political adventurers South into attempted revolution. By complying with this request, you will confer many obligations on your sympathizing fellow-citizens of the North.

Very truly, yours, &c.

AARON L. REID,
HENRY O'RIELLY,
JOHN J. SPEED,
HENRY C. GARDINER,
THOS. LAIDLAW,
ELLIS S. POTTER,
GEORGE N. WILLIAMS,
DANIEL G. FARNHAM,
LORENZO SHERWOOD,
CHAS. P. KIRKLAND,
GEORGE P. NELSON,
THOMAS EWBANK,
E. H. R. LYMAN,
JOSIAH T. LOW,
GEORGE L. MEACHAM,
and others.

REPLY.

METROPOLITAN HOTEL,
NEW YORK, Oct. 1, 1862.

GENTLEMEN: I am in receipt of your note of this date, inviting me to deliver an address at the Academy of Music, in Brooklyn, on next Thursday evening. I accept the invitation and tender my thanks for your kindness and sympathy. Very truly, yours,

A. J. HAMILTON.

AARON L. REID, and others, *Committee.*

The Brooklyn Academy of Music was thronged accordingly by an enthusiastic audience eager to welcome the eminent Union refugee from Texas, the Hon. A. J. HAMILTON, ex-Member of Congress from that State, who had been invited to speak on The Cause, the Consequence, and the Cure of the Rebellion. The stage was crowded with the leading citizens of the Sober City. Mr. Hamilton was introduced by A. A. Low, Esq. He was received with loud and prolonged applause.

MR. HAMILTON said: Ladies and Gentlemen of Brooklyn, at the threshold of the remarks that I shall submit to you this evening upon the gravest subject which in my judgment has ever yet addressed itself to a free people, permit me to say, in one word, I thank you for this reception. [Cheers.] I thank you, fellow-citizens (permit me to call you), not because of personal gratification at the manifestation you made this evening of your loyalty, and your appreciation of loyalty in others, but because, if you will allow the expression, it will be received, if indeed it shall ever reach them, by thousands as loyal as I, in my distracted country, as a just and proper compliment to them also. [Cheers.]

We have come to ascertain, if we can, why our country is in this condition, the causes, the remedies to be applied, and that too without the fear of offense, save the fear which resulted from the dread of offending against truth. [Cheers.]

The Union for the time being is dismembered, and why? Here I find, as well as elsewhere, a great many who can give the cause, and reference is made constantly to some past political principle woven into the policy of the Government by this or that party. Another will attribute the disasters which have overtaken the Government to another party. I meet with men every day who can convince me, as they suppose, that the Abolitionists of the North were the cause of the Rebellion, or that the Democratic party was the cause, or that it resulted from a mistake on the part of our fathers, who framed the Government, in not incorporating wise provisions that would have prevented a contest between the two sections of the country.

I will not, at my time of life, in the sere and yellow leaf, and when so much is before us to accomplish the salvation of the country and the perpetuity of its institutions, in which the liberties of the people are involved, attempt—there is too little time left me for that work—to spend any of it in listening longer than enough to manifest decent respect to any twaddle about the cause of the rebellion.

I say, what are you going to do about it? The fact is that the rebellion exists. You will agree with me that a great, paternal, glorious Government, is being sacrificed—that, if the effort to destroy is be successful, we may well doubt whether we or our children will ever be the recipients of the same measure of freedom and the blessings resulting from good Government that we have been.

Then, the only question for you and I is, to determine the mode of restoring the Government.

It is too late to ask, but perhaps well enough to inquire, what were the causes of this rebellion.

I cannot do better than to call your attention to what one of the leading spirits (a Mr. Spratt, of South Carolina, who addressed a communication at great length, and, as he intended, with consummate ability, replete with all the arguments of the school to which he belonged) could bring to bear upon the principles upon which their Government was to be based, as contrasted with the Government of the United States.* He said there was *no man who deserved the name of statesman in the South, who would pretend that Secession was caused by any aggression of the North upon the rights of the people of the South.* He said it was still less the result of any act of oppression on the part of the United States Government. What then was the reason? He said it was because of the difference in the organization of society North and South. It was because in the non-slaveholding States, from the fact that every man was a freeman, you were necessarily Democratic; every man being a freeman, it resulted that the laboring class in the non-slaveholding States had the power in the Government, and it required but little argument to prove that when that was the case, the Government was in the heels of society, because labor was always in excess of the direction of labor; that is to say, there were more laboring men, and there would continue to be, than there were men who by means of their capital directed labor. He said when Government was in the hands of those who direct labor alone, it was in the head of society, where it properly belonged. And now, said he, having cut loose from the North, have we eradicated the evil? Have we succeeded in gaining our object? Not at all.

He was explaining in this letter that the Government at Montgomery, Ala., had failed in meeting the objects of the revolution, because it had not provided for reopening the African slave-trade. Said he, it will involve the necessity of another revolution. Here is the evil; here are the laboring men, and they are in the majority, too, who wield the power in the Government. They vote at the ballot-box, and from the premises that I have laid down you will perceive that slavery and Democracy are incompatible. [Loud cheering.]

He paid a high compliment to the great New York statesman who is now the Secretary of State of the United States Government [cheers], and said that that great statesman, for he gave him credit for being great, never uttered a greater truth than when he said there was an irrepressible conflict between the two systems of society. [Great applause.] And, said he, in this additional, this second revolution, that will be forced upon us, although it may be bloodier than the one in which we are now engaged, *we must get rid of the last and the least remains of Democracy*, and, to use the least plain and emphatic of his words, we must have *a slave aristocracy.*

Well, fellow-citizens, if that was the sentiment of one solitary man in the South, if it had not been addressed by one of the leading spirits engaged in rebellion, to another, the trusted agent of the State of Louisiana, then a sitting member of the attempted new Government, there might be but little significance in it. If it had been reprobated by the public press of that country, if it had been condemned by the public voice—and when I say the public voice, I mean that of those who wield the power of the South, whose voice alone is heard—it might have gone for nothing; but when you bear in mind that that letter was reproduced in the leading press of the South, spoken of in terms of commendation, and no man has to this day uplifted his voice against any one of the positions there assumed—if you could, as I have done, hear in the hotels, and in the streets, and in parlors, echoes of that sentiment from men who, two years ago, were regarded as loyal, saying, *Republicanism is a failure*—we are astonished that we ever thought it could succeed; we now realize the fact that we must have a stronger Government—if you knew it as I know it, you would feel, fellow-citizens, that there was something more involved in this revolution than a simple desire to get rid of this hated Yankee.

It is not because the men who inaugurated it hated the people of the North. As Mr. Spratt says, it was not because they felt that you had seriously wronged them, but it was a deliberate purpose on their part to be the controlling spirits in a new and a different order of Government, where their power would be perpetual, and they would not be subjected to the chances of the free choice of a free people in recurring elections, as had been the case in past time in our country; and he that does not realize that fact to-day, does not yet understand what that revolution means, and by consequence *the man that is to-day flattering himself that, by conciliatory measures, by kind words, by peace offerings,* the disloyal States can be caused to resume their position in the Confederacy, *is wofully deceived;* it never will happen in that way. [Cheers.] There is but one remedy, and that is on the physical power of the loyal people of the North—[Great applause]—the physical power, directed by the exercise of sufficient thought to lead you to just conclusions as to what the consequences are to be to you as well as to the balance of the people of the United States in case of failure.

And I would say to you, fellow-citizens, that I speak in behalf of the suffering people of the South, who are the great body politic of the South, saving and excepting the office-holders, for all have suffered, not only in respect of business, commerce—by the destruction of confidence between man and man, the utter annihilation of the protection of wise and salutary laws—but the upheaving of the very elements of society as well—all have suffered in that respect; I speak of the whole body politic.

Whatever may be said of what I say here to-night, I know I have not yet passed through the last ordeal of trial in consequence of these troubles. It was hard to part with friends of years; it was hard to give up the position,

* Further illustrations of this important subject will be found in the address from the Democratic League, entitled "The Plottings of Rebellion—The Issue in its Magnitude"—republished on page 10.

whatever it may have been, which I had enjoyed; it was hard to part with wife and children; it was hard to leave home without knowledge that I would ever return. But I had something to sustain me in this—I had true and loyal friends, who gave me moral aid and comfort; it may be that some of these may fall away from me now, because my mind may be led to a conclusion which they are not yet prepared for, but to which they are just as certain to arrive as I have arrived at it to-night.

Mr. Spratt says, then, that this revolution was not because the spirit of the Northern people was aggressive, it was not the Government of the United States was aggressive, but *because the very framework of society here would*, if left free to grapple with slavery, *destroy it by moral force.*

Whether that view is the precise one that has influenced those who have engaged in the rebellion of the South or not, they have been sufficiently convinced of one fact, that the influence of non-slaveholders in the new Government was to be felt less and less year by year, until at last they should be reduced to the condition of serfs, and that *the slaveholder*, and he alone, *should govern the country.*

Now, while two years ago I would not have lent my aid to a man who was seeking the destruction of slavery—while I would have regarded him as an impracticable friend of the Government and the peace of society—while I dreaded to see an appeal which would bring in collision the spirit which opposed slavery with slavery—while I did believe that our fathers who framed the Government understood well how to avoid trouble on the one hand and inevitable difficulty on the other. I am not prepared to see that system used for the purpose of perpetuating itself, and, in the same ratio that it is elevated, my children depressed. The question has been changed. It is not what it was two years ago. There was no party then who sought more than simply to protect slavery under the laws, and when the experiment of secession was being entered upon, I said to them: Do not enter upon it. If you do, you will inevitably destroy the institution; it *is laying the knife to the throat of slavery.* You are in the habit of saying that I am not sound upon the subject. I would save you from the very influence which you pretend to dread. You cannot, against the moral force and power of all Christendom, sustain that institution, saving and excepting under the protection of the United States Government. [Cheers.] It is because the opposition to it elsewhere throughout the world, in view of the immeasurable blessings the United States Government is affording to humanity, dare not, on account of that one blot, if they conceive it to be so, attack the integrity of that Government; but when you shall have risked the alternative of destroying that Government for slavery, *and seek to build a Government upon slavery, as its chief corner-stone*, you then challenge the public opposition of the world to it, and you will inevitably fall under it. You cut loose from thousands of loyal friends. I mean not men who would, if it were proposed now for the first time, help you make it, but men who respect the Constitution of the United States as they understand it—respect laws, respect the good neighborhood and peace that we enjoy as citizens of a great and glorious Republic. They believe that there is some ameliorating power in the All-wise Providence that will allow the remedy to be applied sooner or later, when it is felt to be an intolerable evil. But you have not waited for this; you have determined, against the public sense of the world, to sacrifice all these considerations *—resolving to have no power but slavery alone;* you do more than that, because, with whatever purpose you commence, you will find that you have not progressed two or three years before, in your own judgment, it will be an impossibility to make the new Government liberal. The reasons, fellow-citizens, are obvious. Sooner or later it will be demonstrated that *the great body politic of the people of the South were loyal to this Government*, and did desire to preserve it. [Cheers.] The question at once arises, why, then, did they suffer themselves to be forced out of the Union?

It is much more difficult to make one who was not present understand this, than one who was present. Every artifice was used. Minds had been poisoned through a long series of years. It had got to be a fashion to out-Herod Herod in maintaining that not only was slavery a divine institution, but one of the brightest evidences of the perfection of that wisdom that created all good—[Laughter]—and even those whose mission it ought to have been to spread the doctrine of peace on earth and good-will toward men, to spend their time in the pulpit proving that it was an institution ordained of God. I have about the same opinion of some in the North who spent their time in proving that it originated in hell. [Laughter.] My simple, unregenerate view of the subject was, that God knows best, and that it was permitted, for some wise, inscrutable purpose; and that, when that had been accomplished, it would, by the very same power, cease. The public mind was poisoned. The argument was: The only way you can stop the Northern people, is to go out of the Union; and if you go out now they will soon begin to beg for your own terms for reconstruction.

That was the argument employed everywhere, and thousands upon thousands of men were induced to go to the ballot-box and vote for secession, having been made to believe that it would be the means of securing perpetual peace.

But, again, others who had thought naturally upon the subject would say to their Union fellow-citizens: Do not go to the polls. What have you to do with this movement? It is revolutionary; it is unauthorized; it is a proceeding to which you ought not, by any participation, to give your countenance. Let the madmen, who are seeking the ruin of the State, go to the polls alone.

So in many of the States not a third of the vote of the State was cast. That was the case in my own State. In Louisiana it is now known that there were a majority of the votes cast against secession. At many of the polls were posters saying: "Let the vote be open, that we may see who are the traitors,"—and the Union-men dared not vote.

You may say that these Union-men did not care for their liberty so much as their fathers did. Gentlemen, most of us prefer reading about martyrs to being martyrs; and I would myself rather be a martyr in some other way than to have a rough rope put around my neck, and be hung on a lonely prairie, and have my body left there unburied.

You ask, has this happened? Aye, fellow-citizens, it has happened; it is happening every day; it will continue to happen until the last free spirit has left the South, or his soul has been crushed, unless the power of this Government steps in. [Cheers.] It commenced before secession was commenced. In my own State it commenced pending the presidential canvass in which Mr. Lincoln was elected. I was not present when any one of these victims fell. I did not have the honor of belonging to any vigilance committee, nor was I member of any K. G. C., but I take the evidence of the men engaged in it, published in the public newspapers, for the fact that more than 200 men perished thus because they were suspected of loving their children more than they loved their neighbor's negroes. [Sensation.]

If, then, the necessity of that institution requires such support, *they have severed my allegiance* (if ever I had any) *to it.* [Cheers.]

Nor will the men who have compelled me to leave my State be at all disappointed at what I say here or elsewhere. I advised them in advance that if they would force upon me the issue of infidelity to the Government of my childhood and of my father before me—infidelity to that, or infidelity to Slavery—my choice was easily made. [Applause.] If they compelled me to elect between my children and their negroes, a fool could tell where I would be found. [Cheers.]

That issue is before you, fellow citizens, to-night. It is upon me; it is upon every man from Maine to Mexico—shirk it, if you can.

Mr. Hamilton gave a striking picture of the changed condition of the non-slaveholding man of the South, and the terrible system of espionage and Lynch-law which had been established throughout the South. He spoke of the difficulties of getting away to a Union man, which were almost insurmountable.

It was a fashionable thing to say, "I am for the Constitution as it is, and the Union as it was." [Cheers.]

The Constitution as it is—Yes. The Union as it was—No! [Loud and prolonged cheering.] He would thank no man to aid him in restoring the Union as it existed in the State of Texas in 1861.

If he were to be martyred for expressing the opinions which Washington expressed, no such Union for him.

Now, he alleged, that the issue was deliberately tendered, of *slavery on one side,* and *freedom for the white race* upon the other.

He spoke on behalf of the once enfranchised free white man of the South. Whether slavery was compatible with Democracy or not, the leaders of the rebellion *intended to save slavery,* whether Democracy was saved or not.

If we did not accept the issue, it would be forced upon us.

The liberties of the North were inseperably bound up with those of the South. If secession should become an accomplished fact, *he could see no safety for republicanism on this continent.*

He believed, too, that we must soon see that republicanism should be maintained, even at the hazard of a foreign war, clear down to the Isthmus. We must not permit poor Mexico to become the victim of Louis Napoleon. [Cheers.] The 80,000 troops going to Mexico were not for Mexico alone. The Mexicans were aware of that, and their prayers were earnestly going up for the salvation of the Government of the United States in all its integrity, and to the utmost extent of its territory, where its jurisdiction ever did exist. [Cheers.]

The Government hereafter must have as much power as it had before, and use it better.

Mr. Hamilton concluded by a striking picture of the imbecility with which the rebellion was treated by Buchanan, and by exhorting all to strengthen the hands of the Government, the Government of an honest President, and to concentrate all its energies upon the crushing of the rebellion. He conjured the people of the North to rise to the hight of this great argument. With one united effort let us give to the President and his Generals our hearty and cordial support, with the determination that if they fail, they shall not have to complain of any want of cordial support on our part.

Standing for the first time on free soil, he might be permitted to ask with Webster, that if Freedom should fall, if fall it must, it should fall in the midst of the proud monuments it had reared. [Loud and prolonged applause.]

Mr. Griffiths presented a series of resolutions, thanking Mr. Hamilton for his address, and, after a few words from the Hon. Mr. Odell, in which he pledged the last man and the last dollar of Brooklyn and the North to put down and crush out the rebellion forever the immense audience separated.

COL. HAMILTON'S SECOND SPEECH

ON THE CAUSES AND OBJECTS OF THE REBELLION.

THE ARISTOCRATIC ARM OF THE REBELLION.

In response to an invitation of the National War Committee, the Hon. A. J. Hamilton, the eloquent Union refugee from Texas, delivered an address in the large Hall of Cooper Institute last evening (Oct. 4). The hall was densely filled. Upon the platform were David Dudley Field, the Hon. Hiram Walbridge, Prof. Francis Lieber, the Rev. Henry M. Field, Profs. J. J. Owen and Roswell C. Hitchcock, Brig.-Gen. Strong, S. B. Chittenden, and others. At 7½ o'clock Gen. Hiram Walbridge called the meeting to order. He said—

FELLOW-CITIZENS: The National War Committee have assigned to me the duty of calling to order this vast patriotic and intelligent assemblage. Without office, without honors, without emoluments, without patronage, they trace their authority only in the rectitude of their intention, in the imminence of public danger, and they fondly trust in the regard and esteem of their countrymen. [Cheers.] No sane man believes that this gigantic rebellion, which fairly shakes the earth beneath our feet, can ever be quelled unless the Federal Government shall furnish the opportunity for the loyal patriotic Union men of the South to demonstrate their valor, their intrepidity, their devotion to the Constitution, the Union, and the supremacy of law. [Applause.] That Constitution and the Government it guarantees sprung from the hearts of the American people. It was baptized in their blood, and it will be defended by their hands so long as treason shall seek to ignore that flag that has borne the glories of the American character into every part of the habitable globe. [Great applause.] I take the liberty, therefore, gentlemen, of respectfully nominating as presiding officer upon the occasion, our eminent chief magistrate, the Hon. George Opdyke. [Loud and prolonged applause.]

Mayor Opdyke said: My friends, we are here to listen to a distinguished citizen of the South, a friend of the Union, and of the old flag, who has been compelled to flee from the iron despotism which the confederate traitors have established there. It is therefore that we are favored with the opportunity of obtaining information from that region from a source at once so trustworthy, so enlightened, and so eloquent. Tho orator of the evening is a gentleman of distinguished social position, and eminent public service, having represented his State in the Congress of the United States with marked ability, and I trust the day is not far distant when he will again be called upon to serve his fellow-citizens in the same capacity. I present to you the Honorable A. J. Hamilton, of Texas. [Enthusiastic and continued applause.]

Mr. Hamilton said: Fellow-citizens of the City of New York, could I, by the exercise of some supernatural power, present to those I left behind the scene upon which I now gaze, and bring back the answer which springs in every heart that throbs with a loyal feeling, you would be thanked as alone would be fitting for this overpowering welcome.

I remember well, as I entered your magnificent harbor but a few days past, for the first time in my life, I could but be impressed with the evidence before me of the magnitude, the progress, and the greatness of our country, as represented upon but one single spot of its country.

But there was connected with it a painful throb, and it arose from the reflection that all that was now being imperiled; and whatever you, fellow-citizens, may have supposed with regard to the progress of this rebellion, or the extent, so far as territory is concerned, or the integrity of the people of any section of the country—satisfied as you may be in your own minds that it could not go beyond the States of the South—I entertain a different opinion. I mean to be understood, if it is to succeed where it is already attempted, in my humble judgment it will not stop there; in short, that if the Government of the United States, as it existed before the rebellion, is not maintained in all its integrity, we may look forward to a period, perhaps not so remote that some here present will not see it, when it will give way here also.

Mr. Hamilton proceeded to investigate the cause of the rebellion. Had the theory now advanced throughout the South, that *Republicanism was a failure*, been put forth at the commencement of the rebellion, it would have been nipped in the bud. But when the arms and the powder and lead were all concentrated in the hands of the Government, they raised the cry: "*Democracy is a failure.* You perceive it is a failure, because the United States Government has failed. We must get rid of the people of the North because they are democratic. Slavery and Democracy cannot live together." [Loud and prolonged applause.]

The only reply which he made, so long as he could make any, to these statements as to the weakness of Democracy, was: "Gentlemen, by the time you have got through with Uncle Sam you will find it strong enough for common use." [Loud cheers.] He had been what was called a loyal man to the institution of slavery, but the moment the old flag was torn down he had told them that they would make him not only an Abolition sympathizer, but an active, practical Abolitionist. [Enthusiastic cheering.]

He feared that there were those here who still fancied that by some conciliatory measures the South could be brought back to the old Government. There could be no greater fallacy. [Applause.] The loyal men of the South were praying to get back into the Union without any condition or conciliation. Would any loyal men consent that Jeff. Davis should ever be President of the United States. ["No, no."] Mr. Hamilton continued: "I do want to see the old Government, when it shall have asserted its power, make a wise and just discrimination between the guilty and the deluded. [Cheers.] I want the really responsible traitors punished. [Applause.] I want the downtrodden, the suffering, the ignorant, to be allowed to come back like the prodigal son, and be forgiven. [Cheers.]

If we cannot conciliate these men what can we do? Shall history record it that twenty-seven millions of freemen, and women, and children have not the moral and physical power to strangle treason in fifteen hundred thousand? Is republicanism to fail upon this continent because that twenty-seven millions are not sufficiently conscious of their duty to themselves, to the Government of their fathers, to humanity the wide world over, to realize the fact that this rebellion can alone be crushed by physical force?

I have not a doubt but peace propositions will come from the Confederate Government, but they will not come in the shape of an unconditional proposition to assume the Union as it was, leaving the elective franchise as it was.

We have already seen some of the conditions, or what would probably be the conditions, if hostilities were to cease. I do not think that they even would emanate from the Cabinet—if I may be allowed the expression—at Richmond. They know that if the Government of the United States should, in its mercy, pardon their offenses, and restore them to their rights under the Constitution, their own fellow-citizens who have been their victims would spurn them away, and they are as effectually cut off from preferment as if they had been convicted of high treason. The very desperation with which they are struggling ought to prove to you and the world that they will never stop while they can get men to bleed; they will never cease to fight as long as there is a hope of success, because it is the only hope of salvation to them. They do not feel for the sufferings of the wives and the children that are made widows and orphans by this unholy war; it never has entered the mind of one man in this rebellion, who understood its objects, to shed a tear for all the bloodshed, misery and woe which it involved.

The war must be put down by bayonets, by powder and ball, by brave hearts and strong arms. [Cheers.]

I do not say this because I have suffered; it is because thousands of brave men are suffering now. It is true, had I not suffered and witnessed suffering, I might not, and probably would not, have been so earnest in my feelings. We are all sufficiently selfish, and I am no exception.

If secession is an accomplished fact, and the Government that has resulted from it an established Government among the nations of the earth, do you believe that secession would stop there? Are there not men even in the Empire State, in your goodly city, who would listen to treason? [Wood, Wood, Wood.] There may be no such men in all New York, but, fellow-citizens, I would dislike exceedingly to think that my hopes of the future depended upon the fact of there being no such men. [Laughter.]

I say that I do not question the loyalty of the great heart of New York. I mean that man has not, even here in New York, attained to human perfectability. There are men doubtless here who would be willing to be the great particular magnates here in New York, at the expense of the Government at Washington. [Cheers.]

It is certain to my mind that, once it is established that it is a possible thing to tear asunder the States, there will be men tugging at it day by day and year by year, and you will not have the confidence you once had that these attacks should be resisted; and you may be led to ask whether, to escape anarchy at last, you had not better have a stronger Government.

There is safety for us and fallen humanity throughout the world in the preservation of the Government of our fathers. [Loud cheers.]

We have confidence in the flag which floats over the soil of New York to-day, but when the one shall have been destroyed, and the other be trailing in the dust, what confidence shall we have in equal success?

I at home felt that I was a degraded man, because I was a son of the South, and the people with whom I had lived so long had forfeited their birthright, and turned away from me, and I was too big a coward to make myself a martyr. I was compelled to leave my home under circumstances painful at any time. The Angel of Death had just passed over my house. But why should I be allowed to remain and weep with my wife over the tomb of a little daughter—I, an old wretch, who dared to tell my neighbors that the solemn oath I had taken to support the Constitution of the United States was still binding? I had done too much to be permitted to live peaceably at home. I had robbed no man in the land; there were those who at times I had fed, and they were first to cry—"Crucify him! Hang him!"

In Mexico there are now 500 men who left as I left. They are in the mountain fastnesses, hunted like wolves. Are they to have help? Give them a chance, and they will bleed for their country, die for it, redeem it; and there are men enough there to-day to redeem it if they were organized and had arms in their hands. Let no man be permitted to live in the Government who will dare again to strut his little hour upon any stage and preach treason to his fellow-men. [Cheers.]

Restore the Government, its Constitution, and its laws to all, fellow-citizens? With all my heart. Restore the Union as it existed for the year just preceding the rebellion? God forbid. [Loud, prolonged, and repeated applause.]

Am I to be remitted back to the soil of Texas, to be hunted by assassins the little remnant of my life? ["No, no!"] Am I to go there to teach my little son that the chief blessing of his great future is to run from street to street and from man to man, and insist that he is as sound a man upon this subject of slavery as lives? [Cheers.] Am I to see my neighbors and friends hung by the neck because they have doubted that the chief business of the Great Ruler of the Universe is not in directing and controlling and maturing and perpetuating the institution of slavery? [Cheers.]

No, fellow-citizens; if I cannot go there and strike hands with my friends at home; if I cannot be again united with my family, except upon the terms that I am to live in such society as existed there, hard as it is to utter, I can find it in my heart to say, let me never see them. But if you mean, by the restoration of the Union as it was, a restoration of that Union such as our fathers intended it to be, then, with all my heart, let us have it. [Great applause.]

The issue is simple; it is plain; the wayfaring man must read it as he runs, though he be a fool—*slavery on the one hand,* and *liberty on the other.* [Loud applause.]

And yet, fellow-citizens, for these brief desultory words, honestly spoken, I am yet to be further tried. Friends doubtless who have stood up for me hitherto, will say they are not prepared for this yet. But I fear not for them; they will arrive in due time where I stand; and I will add, even at the expense of being considered arrogant, if you please, that what I have said to-night, all uninteresting as it may be to you, will strike a chord deep in the hearts of my people.

I know how the people feel, their modes of thought, to what conclusions their minds have already been brought. It is "your negroes, my children." I love my children best—I do not intend to part with the hopes that I have predicated upon my little son. He has, or ought to have—he did have until you took it away from him—the right to aspire to the highest honors in his country's gift. He shall have it. I will fight that my son may be free, even at the expense of freeing your negroes. [Cheers.]

Let me, then, fellow-citizens, indulge the hope that, if it shall be my fortune again to visit home and friends, I can say, and say it truthfully, I am a freeman—I am not merely a theoretical freeman—I have the Constitution of the United States guaranteeing me my freedom; but I have what is dearer still—I have countrymen, I have society, I have brethren, fellow-citizens, all over the State, without an exception, who intend that I shall practice as a freeman throughout my life. They intend that I shall indulge the noblest right that can be given to man—the right of thought, and of impressing my thoughts, humble though they be, upon the minds of others.

If I can go home with that kind of freedom, I want it; less than that I shall never be satisfied with. [Cheering.] Hundreds of men have perished because they had thought, because they had loved freedom, and indulged occasionally in speculations as to how freedom was best to be preserved; they have been hung like felons. I want that to cease. I want the Government of the United States to treat every man in the land as its enemy who will attempt to impose further restrictions upon the right of a free people to think and to talk. [Cheers.] When I see that, then I can lift my hands and say: Blessed, indeed, is this Government! Then I can accept that flag as the emblem of freedom, really, unqualifiedly—having gained new lustre by the very struggle in which its citizens are engaged to-day.

I will indulge the hope that victory upon the field may not only perch upon the standards of our arms, but that a moral halo will surround it from the consciousness of those who are fighting that they are struggling to sustain liberty and to crush the last remains of slavery. [Enthusiastic applause.]

Let then our last thought upon Government and society be: I am yet a citizen of a free Government; I still occupy the position of a recipient of the largest rational human liberty; I am yet on freedom's soil, with freedom's banner floating o'er me. [Loud and continued applause.]

The Hon. Hiram Walbridge then offered the following resolution:

Resolved, That the earnest and cordial thanks of the loyal citizens of New York are hereby tendered to Col. Hamilton for his clear, concise, and thorough exposition of the infamy of the present wicked rebellion, and that it is the duty of the Federal Government at the earliest practicable moment to furnish such aid to the loyal Union men of the South as will enable them again to enjoy all the blessings of representative constitutional government.

The Rev. Dr. Hitchcock, in seconding the resolution, said that never in his life had he been more happy not to have been a conditional man than to-night. They had listened to a Southern slaveholder who happened not to be a rebel, and that Southern slaveholder happened to be an Abolitionist. The one thing to do was to march the loyal millions over every acre of the South, where they would see that this Satanic power sat enthroned on a sacred throne which was as black as night.

The resolution was unanimously adopted, and the meeting adjourned amid loud calls for favorite speakers.

THE PLOTTINGS OF REBELLION.

THE ISSUE IN ITS MAGNITUDE.

Eleven years ago, a leading spirit of Virginia addressed a leading spirit of South Carolina, and distinctly presented the great issue of to-day. The following letter, written in 1851, by Mr. Garnett, then a member of the Virginia Convention sitting to revise the Constitution of the State, to Mr. Trescott, of South Carolina, afterwards Assistant Secretary of State under Mr. Buchanan, is fully significant of the matured designs of the secessionists. This letter was captured at the residence of Mr. Trescott, on Barnwell's Island, and contains the reasonings and motives of the traitors who inaugurated the rebellion. The meaning of the letter is clear on its face. It needs no commentary. We ask our fellow-Democrats to read and ponder it. As Democrats, WE accept the issue as the TRAITORS THEMSELVES understand it—as WE understand it, and as the leading rebels who control the South have FORCED it on the nation—SLAVERY AND DEMOCRACY INCOMPATIBLE! Which shall go under? Let true Democrats answer the question.

LORENZO SHERWOOD,
HENRY O'RIELLY,
CHARLES P. KIRKLAND,
GEO. P. NELSON,
THOMAS EWBANK,
JOHN J. SPEED,
HENRY C. GARDINER,
Corresponding Committee of the Democratic League.

NEW YORK, Sept. 20, 1862.

Letter from Mr. Garnett, of Virginia, to Mr. Trescott, of South Carolina.

"VA. CONVENTION, May 3d, 1851.

"My Dear Sir: You misunderstood my last letter if you supposed that I intended to visit South Carolina this Spring. I am exceedingly obliged to you for your kind invitations, and it would afford me the highest pleasure to interchange, in person, sentiments with a friend whose manner of thinking so closely agrees with my own. But my engagements here closely confine me to this city, and deny me such a gratification.

"I would be especially glad to be in Charleston next week, and witness your Convention of Delegates from the Southern-Rights Associations. The condition of things in your State deeply interests me; her wise foresight and manly independence have placed her at the head of the South, to whom alone true-hearted men can look with any hope or pleasure. Momentous are the consequences which depend upon your action. Which party will prevail? the immediate secessionists, or those who are opposed to separate State action at this time? For my part, I forbear to form a wish. Were I a Carolinian, it would be very different; but when I consider the serious effects the decision may have on your future weal or woe, I feel that a citizen of a State which has acted as Virginia, has no right to interfere, even by a wish.

"If the General Government allows you peaceably and freely to secede, neither Virginia nor any other Southern State would, in my opinion, follow you at present. But what would be the effect upon South Carolina? Some of our best friends here supposed that it would cut off Charleston from the great Western trade which she is now striking for, and would retard very greatly the progress of your State. I confess that I think differently. I believe thoroughly in our own theories, and that if Charleston did not grow quite so fast in her trade with other States, yet the relief from Federal taxation would vastly stimulate your prosperity. If so, the *prestige* of the Union would be destroyed, and you would be the nucleus for a Southern Confederation at no distant day.

"But I do not doubt, from all I have been able to learn, that the Federal Government would use force, beginning with the form most embarrassing to you, and least calculated to excite sympathy—I mean a naval blockade. In that event, could you withstand the reaction feeling which the suffering commerce of Charleston would probably manifest? Would you not lose that in which your strength consists, the union of your people? I do not mean to imply an opinion. I only ask the question. If you could force this blockade, and bring the Government to direct force, the feeling in Virginia would be very great. I trust in God it would bring her to your aid.

"But it would be wrong in me to deceive you by speaking certainly. I cannot express the deep mortification I have felt at her course this Winter. But I do not believe that the course of the Legislature is a fair expression of the popular feeling. In the east, at least, the great majority believe in the right of secession, and feel the deepest sympathy with Carolina in opposition to measures which they regard as she does. But the west—Western Virginia—there is the rub! Only 60,000 slaves to 494,000 whites! When I consider this fact, and the kind of argument which we have heard in this body, I cannot but regard with the greatest fear the question whether Virginia would assist Carolina in such an issue.

"I must acknowledge, my dear sir, that I look to the future with almost as much apprehension as hope. *You well object to the term Democrat. Democracy, in its original philosophical sense, is, indeed, incompatible with slavery, and the whole system of Southern society.* Yet, if we look back, what change will you find made in any of our State constitutions, or in our legislation, in its general course for the last fifty years, which was not in the direction of Democracy? Do not its principles and theories become daily more fixed in our practice?—I had almost said in the opinions of our people, did I not remember with pleasure the great improvement of opinion in regard to the abstract question of slavery. And if such is the case, what have we to hope for the future? I do not hesitate to say that if the question is raised between Carolina and the Federal Government, and the latter prevails, the last hope of Republican Government, and I fear of Southern Civilization, is gone. Russsia will then be a better Government than ours.

"I fear that the confusion and interruption under which I write may have made this a rather rambling letter. Do you visit the North in the Summer? I should be happy to welcome you to the Old Dominion.

"I am much obliged to you for the offer to send me Hammond's Eulogy on Calhoun; but I am indebted to the author for a copy.

"With esteem and friendship,

"Yours truly,

"M. R. H. GARNETT.

"WM. H. TRESCOTT, ESQ."

ANTAGONISTIC PRINCIPLES INVOLVED IN THE REBELLION.

LETTER OF THE DEMOCRATIC LEAGUE TO JOHN BRIGHT.

The following letter from the Executive Committee of the Democratic League, alluding to the antagonisms in which the rebellion originated, has been addressed to John Bright, Manchester, England:

"NEW YORK, August 9, 1862.

"*John Bright, member of the British Parliament.*

"Dear Sir: The Executive Committee of the Democratic League for Sustaining the National Unity, influenced by a just admiration of the character you have earned in this country as well as your own, desire to tender to you the respects and regards of our fellow-countrymen. We do not arrogate too much when we speak in behalf of our fellow-citizens; for, at best, we can but feebly express the kindly sentiments which the millions on this side of the Atlantic entertain towards you.

"It is enough for us to know that you are the warm and firm friend of the masses of your own countrymen. Knowing this, we can appreciate your habits of thought and your readiness to analyze correctly the causes that have led to the present conflict in America. No one who is not imbued with a large and kindly sympathy for the welfare of the masses is competent to be a judge in our matters. There is no other platform than this upon which he can stand and make his survey accurate. Having analyzed society in the United States from the same stand-point that you have contemplated the natural rights of your own countrymen, you have not been mistaken as to the character of the antagonisms which have here culminated in warfare.

"To most people in Europe it must appear surprising that the Americans should have engaged in a civil war of such gigantic magnitude. It could not have been avoided by the Union Government. The two antagonisms of slavery and Democracy had long since entered into the contest. For thirty years or more the rumblings of these discordant elements had gone across the waters. In Europe, where these sounds had reached, the prophecies were made that Democratic Government could not endure. All these unfavorable prophecies were based upon the supposed weakness of the Democratic principle in government. Never was a greater mistake made than this. It has not been the weakness of the Democratic principle, nor its want of adaptation to power in Government, or strength in nationality. It has been the nightmare of slavery that has fastened on the breast of the republic. It was this hideous and disturbing element that created the convulsions of the body politic that have so often seemed to threaten us with dissolution.

"The pro-slavery spirit in politics has not only been the disturber of our domestic peace, but the cause of much reproach to us in Europe. It half paralyzed the principle of civil liberty where it existed. It neglected the general education of the youth. It was ever contumelious in its opposition to the national policy of raising up diversified industry. It had not, and from its nature, could not, have any substantial sympathy in the common welfare of the masses. Selfish, arrogant, and unjust by nature—condemned by a discriminating world for the compound of vices interwoven into its relationships, it has at last, through desperation, taken refuge in the law of force.

"In order to judge with accuracy, it is necessary to understand what brought slaveholders to the desperate resort of attempted revolution. The doctrine was long since promulgated by them that 'a Government of majorities must be abrogated'—'that slavery and Democracy were incompatible'—'that under the operation of the Democratic principle, and the laws of population and subsistence, slavery must soon lose its prestige and go down before the enfranchised masses.' What was to be done? Here was a process of reasoning, founded on foresight of the future, that no argument could turn aside. Statesmen in the North and South concurred in the same conclusion, but with this difference—the one insisting that the democratic principle must be subverted in order to maintain slavery unimpared—the other insisting that the democratic principle in Government must be maintained, though it involved the extinction of slavery. We have now the desperate conflict of arms founded upon the issue thus made.

"Our people of the North dreaded civil war. Every interest had aversion to the resort to arms. Every assurance was given that slavery would not be intermeddled with in states where it existed. Compromises were offered and attempted to be acted on; and everything short of a surrender of the democratic principle in Government was tendered to slaveholders in order to assuage animosity and put back the intended revolution. Our national Government and the party in power did everything possible in conciliatory policy, but with no other result than that of increased determination on the part of slaveholders to persist in the purposes of the rebellion. Slaveholders were not mistaken in their conclusion, that there was a danger to the institution of slavery which no compromises could avert, and against which no party could stipulate or give guaranty. They knew that the frictional contest must soon arise under the laws of population and subsistence. Twenty-three years hence, on the ratio of the past, and the population would be aggregated to sixty millions. Forty-six years would swell it to a hundred and twenty. But a short time in the annals of nationality, and slavery would be crowded by the offshoot of that twenty-seven millions now dependent upon free labor for subsistence, and having every natural motive to political affiliation. This was the mountain of horrors to the pro-slavery sensibilities. This was the political power that politicians could not bind or warp into subordination to the purposes and policy of slavery.

"To glance further at the logic which precipitated the slaveholders into rebellion, they assumed that delay only added to the difficulties of successfully accomplishing a revolution. They had prepared the programme in 1856; and had also arranged for going out of the Union in case Mr. Fremont was elected to the Presidency. The election of Mr. Buchanan at the time merely postponed the attempt, in order to gain additional facilities for success through the treasonable pliancy of his administration. With a traitorous majority in Mr. Buchanan's Cabinet, the work of rebel preparation went rapidly on. Mr. Lincoln's inauguration found it fully prepared for the conflict —almost an overmatch from previous preparation. The nation was taken by surprise, and much time elapsed before the full meaning of the southern conspiracy disclosed itself. It is not fully understood yet by the masses in the United States—much less by the people of Europe. To get at the full meaning of the attempted revolution requires an analysis of the whole reasonings and motives that influenced the slaveholders to enter upon it.

"To the minds of those unacquainted with the reasonings of slaveholders, and their apprehensions excited by the known force of the laws of population, the inquiry naturally arises, "Could not this civil war have been averted?" We assume to know that this war could not have been averted short of surrendering the national Government and the national policy to the dictation of less than three hundred and fifty thousand slaveholders. That this could not be done, and would not be permitted, is now being demonstrated by the democratic masses in arms to maintain the national jurisdiction, and with it the principles of free government.

"We enclose for your perusal a copy of the declaratory resolutions of our League. Also we send by this mail the July number of the *Continental Monthly*, containing an article more fully elucidating the motives and reasonings that led the slaveholders into the attempt at revolution.

"We are aware that the liberalists of Europe have waited with much impatience for the disclosure of a significant policy on the part of our Government towards the institution of slavery. They need not fear on that ground, nor will their just hopes be disappointed. We could have longer tolerated slavery, odious as it is in principle, and damaging as it is to the advancement of civilization, for the sake of peace; but when it openly entered upon *the revilement of the democratic principle*, insisted on *a new order of government*, and commenced the war to throw off the national jurisdiction, it became a very different matter. From that moment *the chain of subordination to its fell influences was broken.* Its prestige has already passed the bounds beyond the pale of restoration. The bill of its abominations is now to be settled through the law of force. What that settlement will be is very plainly foreshadowed in the public sentiment, to the effect that we can neither have peace or become a homogeneous people without removing this gangrene from the body politic.

"Allow us to say a word respecting the distress and depression that have fallen upon the mechanical industry of Great Britain. This result, we are all aware, has grown out of the slaveholders' rebellion. It was a part of the programme that entered into the calculations of the southern conspirators. They openly boasted, in advance, of the misery they could inflict on the laboring classes of England in the management of the incidents when they should have entered upon the rebellion. They verily believed that they could inflict such distress as to bring the Government of Great Britain into alliance with their revolutionary projects. We

COL. HAMILTON, THE LAST DEMOCRATIC CONGRESSMAN FROM TEXAS.

(From an article by Horace Greeley.)

In all the discussions which during a full year preceded and prepared for the President's Proclamation of Freedom, the opponents of Emancipation regarded the alleged repugnance of *Southern* Unionists as their Malakoff. "The Union has too few friends in the South already," they argued: "your policy will deprive it of these few. Aside from the negroes, who are fettered and helpless, the Union will have no remaining well-wishers, in the South after you shall have identified it with Abolition. How can we afford thus to unite the Southern Whites in one compact, determined phalanx against us? It is madness to urge it."

The logic was forcible had the assumption whereon it was based been a fact. But it was not and is not, as every day's developments tend more clearly to establish. The ice is at last broken, and the inundation of Liberal sentiment is already manifest.

Hon. ANDREW J. HAMILTON, of Texas, is a striking illustration of this truth. He is a native of Alabama, reared a slaveholder, always surrounded by slaves, and always regarding Slavery with indolent and unquestioning approval. But for the Rebellion he would probably have died a slaveholder and a reputed admirer of "the peculiar institution."

But Mr. Hamilton, though a slaveholder, was never a disunionist. When he saw those who worked very hard to bring Texas into the Union working even harder to get her out again, and others with her, he stood up to resist them. In 1859, the Democratic party of Texas, with which he had always acted, held a State Convention and nominated H. G. Runnels, formerly Governor of Mississippi, for governor of their State. Runnels was a disunionist; his leading supporters were of the same stripe; the resolves and speeches of the Convention which nominated him smacked of treasonable intent; in short, the nomination was calculated to test the disposition of Texas as to the scheme of a Southern Confederacy. Gen. Sam Houston came out as "stump" candidate for Governor in opposition, and was elected by 8,670 majority—a result to which his prominent connection with the early history of Texas and his personal popularity doubtless contributed. Mr. Hamilton in like manner ran for Congress in the Western District as an independent Union Democrat, and was elected over the regular Democratic candidate, Judge Waul, by 448 majority out of 32,370 votes.

Thus elected to Congress as a Unionist, Mr. Hamilton did not, like John Bell, betray the cause that had honored him. When, in the early part of 1861, his colleague, John H. Reagan, now a member of the Confederate Cabinet, rose to declare his own adhesion and that of his State to the Confederacy, Mr. Hamilton listened till he had concluded, and then said:

"I care not for myself. I made up my mind at the beginning of this trouble never to pause in any exertions because of the condition in which it would place me for the time being, ether here or at home. I have not allowed one single motive of selfishness, if I know my own heart, ever to interfere with the exercise of what little judgment I have been able to bring to bear upon these great questions. I am solemnly impressed, however, Mr Speaker, with the condition in which I actually find myself. In traveling hither from my home, more than two thousand miles distant from this Capital, for the discharge of a public duty, my foot pressed no spot of foreign territory. My eye rested upon not one material object, during my journey, that was not a part and parcel of my country, as I fondly deemed it. When we assembled together, as far as I know, every State and Territory was represented upon this floor. The great fabric of the Government was then complete; but now, how changed! When I go hence, it will be to find my pathway intercepted by new and strange nationalities. Without ever having wandered from my native land, I must traverse foreign countries, if I would return. I might be excused for doubting my own identity. Surely I may be pardoned for having involuntarily prayed that this might prove a troubled and protracted dream. Yet it is too true—too many evidences force conviction of the sad reality. But a few days past, Mr. Speaker, the noble temple of American liberty stood complete in all its parts—stood in all the majesty of its vast proportions, and in the glory of its apparent strength and beauty of construction; not a pillar missing nor a joint dissevered. And its votaries were gathered about the altar, worshiping, as was their wont, with hopeful hearts. Forebodings were felt, and predictions made, of the coming storm, and the destruction of the temple. And the storm has come, and still rages; the temple still stands, but shorn of its fair proportions, and marred in its beauty. Pillar after pillar has fallen away, and while its proud dome still points to heaven, it is reeling in mid-air like a drunken man, while its solid foundations are shaken as with an earthquake. Yet there are worshipers there about the shrine, and I am among them. I have been called by warning voices to come out and escape the impending danger; I have been woed by entreaties and plied with threats. But, sir, neither entreaties, nor threats, nor hope of reward, nor dread of danger, shall tear me away until I lay hold of the horns of the altar of my country, and implore heaven, in its own good time, to still the storm of civil strife, and through such human agency as may be best, again uprear the fallen pillars to their original position, that they may through long ages contribute to the strength and beauty of the noblest structure yet devised by man."

Mr. Hamilton returned to Texas to find her the helpless prey of the Disunion conspirators. The treacherous surrender by Gen. Twiggs of the greater portion of the regular army of the Union (which Floyd had ordered from Utah to Texas, doubtless for that very purpose), had placed in the hands of the active traitors nearly all the arms and ammunition in the State. They were united by a secret league; they were ready for the emergency; and the weakness of Gen. Houston in surrendering the government of the State into their hands, had completed the ruin of the Union cause. For a year or more Mr. Hamilton remained at home, suspected and watched, but not arrested, his character and position being such, that any wanton assault upon him would have redounded to the injury of the Secession cause. During that time, he was advised of repeated instances in which Unionists less conspicuous, and with fewer personal friends than himself, were hunted down, fettered, abused, and slain, for no other offence than that of fidelity to their country. Unionism was everywhere repressed with a strong hand, yet nowhere extinguished. Thousands who were induced to plunge into the black pool of Secession by assurance that it was merely a device to frighten the North into concessions of her rights to the South—by representations that there would be no bloodshed, and that all would be settled and smiling within a few months—have long since been bitterly undeceived by the relentless conscription which has torn every son capable of bearing arms from the paternal hearth, and by the various devices whereby all their stock and crops are swept into the Confederate droves and garners, and paid for in Confederate scrip or not at all. He has no doubt that a majority of the people of Western Texas (with the other half of the State he is comparatively little acquainted) would welcome to-morrow the unfolding among them of the dear old flag under which they always enjoyed abundance, security, and happiness. And Mr. Hamilton, hunted at length from his home, compelled to hide for weeks in the mountains and thickets, and to make his way furtively to the Rio Grande, and thence to Matamoras, New Orleans, and our city, is among us to plead the cause of the Unionists of Texas, who ask that they may be enabled to help themselves. Let them have arms and ammunition, and the nucleus of an army, and they will fill its ranks and joyfully co-operate in crushing out their oppressors, restoring their State to Freedom and the Union.

But Mr. Hamilton, though born, reared, and always living in the Cotton States, is no conditional Unionist. He is openly, unequivocally, in favor of strangling the monster, Slavery, as well as his offspring, Treason—and, recognizing in Slavery at least the fulcrum whereby the traitors were enabled to upset the loyalty of the South, he favors its demolition in order that loyalty may safely rear its head again. Believing that if Slavery were extinguished, the Rebellion would be a fire without fuel, he is a champion of the policy which says, "Let Slavery die, that so the Republic may live." Regarding Secession as *a revolt against democratic institutions*, in order that a narrow oligarchy may monopolize the semblance as well as the reality of power, he would crush out that oligarchy, by abolishing that which gives it unity and prestige, that so Liberty and Union may abide and flourish evermore. Such is Hon. Andrew J. Hamilton of Texas. Do not miss an opportunity to hear him, and let his earnest words fire your heart with a deeper devotion to Freedom and our Country!

THE CAUSE AND CURE OF THE SLAVEHOLDERS' REBELLION.

(From the New York Daily Times.)

Mr. HAMILTON, of Texas, is one of the most earnest prophets the South has yet given to the Union. He has trodden the wine-press of rebel hate, and bears marks of the vassalage sought to be imposed upon him. He stands before his loyal countrymen to-day a martyr to his principles, and his life saved by a miracle, as it were, of good fortune. He was dogged from his home, through the settlements and into the mountains of Texas. Five times his attempt to escape was defeated. He was the mark at which the assassin's bullet was sped. He reached the Gulf coast at last and found safety on shipboard. "The last thing I saw," he says, "on looking back from the schooner's deck to the receding shores of Texas, was the little launch full of armed men who had failed to catch me."

Such is the simple story of Mr. Hamilton's escape from Texas. In leaving that State he was, he says, severing all early connections, parting with life-long friends, giving up his position in society (which was a high and enviable one, we can say for him), breaking the links that bound him to wife and children, and leaving "home," without knowing whether or not he would ever return? Is not that a picture of the cruelest fate that can befall any man in this life? But it represents the price that a brave man pays for his independence in the South.

Surely Mr. Hamilton is authorized to speak on behalf of the Union men of the South. He has done so in this city. He is to do so again; and we only wish he could speak so as to be heard by every free man in New York State. Mr. Hamilton puts an end to many of the miserable quibbles among political partisans about the origin of the war. He says it is false to ascribe the rebellion to the action of the Abolition party. He says, and says truly, that no Southern leader ever yet admitted that slavery was not adequately protected by the National Government. We know that the Confederate Commissioners in Europe have labored most assiduously to convince foreign cabinets that the Northern States were no more disposed to the abolition of slavery than the Southern. But neither, says Mr. Hamilton, did the Democratic party (Mr. Buchanan's Administration) produce the war. The cause was deeper than all the causes assigned. It was the conviction on the part of Southern oligarchs (mainly slaveholders) that *republicanism was a failure*, and their determination to form a Government in which *the labor of the nation should have no representation.*

This is the basis of the rebellion, and this is the battle we are fighting. It is the old battle of freedom against despotism, which, from the beginning, has crimsoned the earth with blood. Mr. Hamilton assures us that the non-slaveholding whites of the South, though misled at first by the scheming authors of the rebellion, are beginning to see that it is their own degradation the oligarchs of the South are seeking. He assures us, as we knew before, that a majority in a number of the seceded States were opposed to the rebellion, and he says that the rebels, since the secession, "have made no friends among the Union men." On the other hand, he declares that the scales have fallen from the eyes of thousands who were in the beginning duped into treason, and that they stand ready to espouse the cause of the old Government. This is, indeed, cheering news, and should reanimate the hope and courage of the loyal millions who are fighting this great and final battle of freedom. We shall have the Union restored—not the "Union as it was," as semi-traitors mouth the phrase—but the Union as Washington and Jefferson left it. The words of Mr. Hamilton on this point contain the convictions of the nation now in arms against the rebellion. The voice of the people will be the voice of God. Laws and Constitutions must yield to the popular right and popular safety. Says Mr. Hamilton:

"I invoke the aid of the loyal people in restoring the Government of the United States. But, fellow-citizens, if you had the power, and were to tender to me to-night the restoration of the Union as it existed in the State of Texas in 1861, I would not thank you for the boon. [Applause.] If, because I cannot measure my conscience or judgment with those of my neighbor, or a majority of my neighbors, I am to be looked upon with coldness, suspicion, and aversion; if I am to be insulted and spit upon by the children of my neighbors whom I may have dandled on my knees, thinking that they would, at least, remember me with kindness as their father's neighbor and friend; if I am to be looked upon as something loathsome, because I cannot believe that Slavery is the beginning and the end of all legitimate government; if, above all, I cannot say what I believe, that there are excesses and abuses in respect to that institution which ought to be looked to; if, in short, because I might say what WASHINGTON said, believing it; what JEFFERSON wrote, and what all the good and great men of that day believed, I am to be stigmatized as a traitor, and made to suffer a traitor's doom; if that is to be the result of the "Union as it was," I want no such Union. [Applause.] If, when the Union is restored, as I trust it will be, I may be at liberty to go out and realize the fact in a practical sense that I am the recipient of the great and inestimable right intended to be secured to me by the Constitution of the United States; if I can enjoy the right of speech as well as the liberty of conscience, then I can bless such a Union; but I cannot bless one which 'holds out the word of promise to the ear to break it to the hope.'"

Mr. HAMILTON does not think that "the South will be ruined" if Slavery is destroyed. He thinks the slaveholders and rebels will be, but that *the non-slaveholders of the South*, who are the great majority of the white people there, *will be happily enfranchised*, set free, enriched and enobled by that event, which crushes the aristocrats and oligarchs. *This is a new view of the subject.* It is a philosophic view taken by a free man of the South, in the interest of the South. It is a view that harmonizes with the emancipation edict of the Government—that annihilates the sophisms of semi-traitors in the North—that kindles the hearts of freemen everywhere to a holy zeal against the selfish tyrants of the rebellion—that gives assurance of a new and a true life for the South after Slavery is overthrown, and guarantees a Union as peaceful and enduring as its leading principles shall be free, humanizing, and eternal.

The Slaveholders' Denunciations against Democracy.

Garnett's letter to Trescott, published on the 10th page, is one of the clearest revelations of the purposes of the Slaveholders in this Rebellion.

That Mr. Trescott was a thorough sympathizer with the Virginian Slaveholder in denouncing Democratic principles, is indicated in various ways, even in his Address before the South Carolina Historical Society, as published in the Charleston Mercury, and re-published in De Bow's Review for December, 1859, wherein he says:

"That the institution [of Slavery], which, with the men of former times, was an experi-
" ment, had become the corner-stone of their social and political life:"

And yet there were some men in South Carolina "who would eradicate our old State
" pride—destroy the conservative character of our State politics—strip us bare of the glorious
" achievements of the past, and drive us, destitute and dishonored, into the *fit companionship*
" *of a vagabond and demoralized Democracy.*"

—And all this denunciation of "Democracy," while Trescott was actually serving as Mr. Buchanan's "Democratic" Assistant Secretary of State—plotting the ruin of our Democratic institutions, because "Slavery is incompatible with Democracy."

SLAVOCRACY AGAINST DEMOCRACY --- THE GREAT CAUSE OF THE REBELLION.

REMARKS OF THE HON. LORENZO SHERWOOD,

Ex-Member of the Texan Legislature,

ON THE COURSE OF THE SLAVEHOLDERS' CONSPIRACY AGAINST DEMOCRATIC GOVERNMENT.

"The leaders in this Rebellion are actuated by a distinct purpose to SUPPLANT POPULAR GOVERNMENT AND ESTABLISH A MONARCHY," with "Slavery as its corner-stone."

When first addressing his northern fellow-countrymen, Col. Hamilton, the last Democratic Congressman from Texas, thus pointed to the cause and the cure of the Rebellion. Referring to the declarations of prominent slaveholders, that they "*must get rid of the last and least remains of Democracy*," Col. H. said:

"If you could, as I have done, hear in the hotels and in the streets, and in parlors, echoes of that sentiment from men who, two years ago, were regarded as loyal, saying, '*Republicanism is a failure*—we are astonished that we ever thought it could succeed; *we now realize the fact that we must have a stronger Government*'—if you knew it as I know it, you would feel, fellow-citizens, that there was something more involved in this revolution than a simple desire to get rid of the 'hated Yankee.' It is not because the men who inaugurated it hated the people of the North—it was not because they felt that you had seriously wronged them—but it was a deliberate purpose on their part to be the controlling spirits in *a new and a different order of Government*, where their power would be perpetual, and they would not be subjected to the chances of the free choice of a free people in recurring elections, as had been the case in past time in our country; and he that does not realize that fact to-day, does not yet understand what that rebellion means, and, by consequence, *the man that is to-day flattering himself that, by conciliatory measures, by kind words, by peace-offerings*, the disloyal States can be caused to resume their position in the Confederacy, *is wofully deceived*—it never will happen in that way. There is but one remedy, and that is in the physical power of the loyal people of the North—the physical power, directed by the exercise of sufficient thought to lead you to just conclusions as to *what the consequences are to be to you*, as well as to the balance of the people of the United States, *in case of failure*."

* * * "I have grown wearied and disgusted with the mawkish sensibility over the negro, when there is so much higher and more available ground to take in favor of the white man," says Lorenzo Sherwood. * * * "My sympathies are enlisted in the great cause of *white humanity in its shirt-sleeves*—of that twenty-seven millions of American free citizens who are bound to the eternal business of subsistence through their own industry. Their lot is to toil—to toil on from generation to generation: and a pretty business it is for less than one hundred thousand slaveholders to set these toiling millions to cutting one another's throats!"

THE SLAVEHOLDERS' REBELLION—ITS ORIGIN AND OBJECTS

The following correspondence, showing the estimate placed on the opinions of the Hon. Lorenzo Sherwood by Col. Hamilton, of Texas, may serve as an introduction to the annexed outlines of the late speech of Mr. Sherwood, in New Jersey, concerning the Origin and Objects of the Slaveholders' Rebellion:

CORRESPONDENCE.

NEW YORK, 32 Pine St., Oct. 18, 1862.

COL. ANDREW JACKSON HAMILTON.

Dear Sir—Knowing the profound interest with which you watch the diffusion of information concerning the real motives influencing the Slaveholders' Conspiracy, I respectfully submit for your consideration a proof-sheet of the outlines of the Hon. Lorenzo Sherwood's late speech in New Jersey, with the belief that an expression of your opinion concerning his statements and reasonings would still further commend them to the consideration of your loyal countrymen South and North, and to the friends of free government in other lands, who wish to know the true causes of the attempted destruction, not only of our National Government, but of democratic institutions, by the slave-aristocracy, at the present crisis.

As no one knows better than you do the opportunities of Mr. Sherwood for learning thoroughly and correctly appreciating all branches of information concerning these vital questions—opportunities afforded by his long Southern experience and his intimate connection with public affairs (in and out of the Legislature) of Texas; and as I know the cordiality with which you and Mr. Sherwood have co-operated in sustaining loyal sentiments in the South, and in endeavoring to cause the true motives of the rebellion to be correctly understood among your Northern fellow-countrymen, as set forth in the publications of the Democratic League, I am sure you will not consider intrusive this request for an expression of your opinion on the above-mentioned points.

Yours, respectfully,

HENRY O'RIELLY.

REPLY.

NEW YORK, OCT. 18, 1862.

MY DEAR SIR:—Your note of to-day, calling my attention to, and asking my opinion of, the facts and arguments contained in a proof-sheet of the outlines of the Hon. Lorenzo Sherwood's late speech in New Jersey, is before me. But a few moments are left me for reply, as I am in the act of leaving the city.

I fully concur in all that is contained in that speech. These are matters not new to either Mr. Sherwood or myself; nor do we now for the first time interchange opinions upon them. Together we have, in years past, watched the inevitable tendency in the South to the present deplorable condition of our country. There are few men of my acquaintance who are so well prepared, from observation, experience and reflection, to think wisely and act justly in the premises as Mr. Sherwood.

Very truly and respectfully,

A. J. HAMILTON.

To HENRY O'RIELLY, Esq.

SPEECH OF LORENZO SHERWOOD,

EX-MEMBER OF THE TEXAN LEGISLATURE,

RESPECTING THE SLAVEHOLDERS' CONSPIRACY AGAINST DEMOCRATIC PRINCIPLES, AS WELL AS AGAINST THE NATIONAL UNION.

MY FREE FELLOW-COUNTRYMEN:

I thus designate you, in contradistinction to the masses in the South, who are now under the sway of despotism, and who are no longer free. Hard as this word is to speak, and painful as it is to contemplate, the declaration is true. Those who have heretofore sympathized with you in the belief that they had enduring free government, and who are attached to its principles, find themselves suddenly transferred to the degradation of a most mercenary and relentless despotism. I come to you to-night to disclose and elucidate the full meaning of the conspiracy that has deprived them of their political rights; to excite your generous sympathy in their behalf; and, if possible, to increase your animated determination to uphold that clause of the Constitution which guaranties to the people of every State "free republican government."

If I arrogate to myself something of special information, and more than is common to most others, it is only for the reason that I have been placed more immediately in contact with those who have co-operated in this great Southern conspiracy, fitly denominated "The Slaveholders' Rebellion." It is a conspiracy, not only against the national jurisdiction, but a most foul conspiracy also against free government in the South. I is this phase of the question that I would discuss, for it is as patent to my mind that a new order of government, based on privilege of class, is intended to be established, as it is that the national jurisdiction has been repudiated. If any one could have seen what I have seen, heard what I have heard, and watched and analyzed what has been thrust upon my attention during my fourteen years' residence in the South, he would have little difficulty in concluding as to the motives of the rebellion.

Whoever is placed in immediate contact with the reasonings of a class, and follows up that course of reasoning through a series of years, will have little difficulty in divining the ulterior motives of that class, however much the attempt may be made to disguise them. The motives will crop out from the line of reasoning. When slaveholders talk against "a government of majorities," it means something. When they talk about the necessity of "abrogating a government of majorities," it swells into significance of something more than idle theory. It means an intended new arrangement of political power. When you see a periodical like De Bow's Review, which is the oracle and organ of the slaveholders, and the sacred depository of the political literature of their class, you may gather from the tenor of its pages something of what is meant. If you never find a generous democratic sentiment on its pages, you may conclude that its authors or contributors do not entertain such sentiments. If you discover that democratic principles are repudiated as vicious in theory and vile in practice, you may know that such principles are objectionable. When you hear the democratic masses reviled, and continuously reviled, in the standard political literature of a class, you may know that those masses are condemned by that class as an objectionable political element. I had every reason to believe, and did believe before secession, that the object of the slaveholders was to overthrow the democratic principle.

When the rebellion actually took place, it revived in my mind many things, previously spoken by slaveholders, that would otherwise have been forgotten. It was then that the many and repeated declarations I had heard through a series of years assumed a significant meaning that dispelled all doubt. Later revelations only tended to confirm the foregone conclusion as to the intent of the slaveholders—that is, the abrogation of democratic government in the South.

As an additional evidence of the plot to secede, as well as the motive, the real, secret motive for secession, I will read the letter of Mr. Garnett to Mr. Trescott, written in 1851. (The speaker here read the letter.) This letter has a most important bearing and most portentous meaning. It was written in secret confidence. It was written by a leading traitor to a leading traitor. It was written just after the Nashville Convention of 1850, where the plot to secede, as is now ascertained, was adopted and determined on. It was written in answer to a treasonable letter, with the sentiments of which Mr. Garnett sympathized. "You well object to the term Democrat," says Mr Garnett: "Democracy is, indeed, incompatible with slavery and the whole system of Southern society." This was a truth which had become patent to the minds of slaveholders, and very few at this time, I think, are prepared to dispute the proposition. Whoever undertakes to controvert the proposition, will be at issue with the political influences now controlling the South.

As far back as 1855, in the July number of De Bow's Review, we find an article written by an eminent Southerner, containing the following reasonings and postulates. Speaking of the Democratic theory, he says: "At the bottom of this theory lies the idea that might makes right; in other words, that a majority of the members of society has a natural, indefeasible, and absolute right to govern the minority. * * * The majority of numbers is more powerful than the Czar, because it is *physical right*. It is more grinding in its tyranny, because it has less feeling of personal responsibility, and its Argus eyes can search every corner of the country. Its infallibility is less open to attack than the Pope's, because it is, itself, public opinion." The author assumes that "in England the ability in government has been preserved by a highly aristocratic Constitution, both social and political."

It may not be unprofitable, in elucidation of this subject, to recite in addition a few declarations and postulates from the present philosophers of the South. I would take up those whose opinions have passed current, and are in conformity with the designs of treason. Mr. George Fitzhugh, of Va., has more than emulated South Carolina in the expression of his motives to get rid of the Union. In the February number of De Bow's Review, 1861, he assumes "that it is a great mistake to suppose that abolition alone was the cause of dissension between the North and the South." He assumes "that the Cavaliers, Jacobites, and Huguenots, who settled the South, naturally hate, contemn, and despise the Puritans who settled the North. The former are master races; the latter, a slave race, the descendants of Saxon serfs. The former are Mediterranean races, descendants of the Romans; for Cavaliers and Jacobites are of Norman descent, and the Normans were of Roman descent, and so were the Huguenots. The Saxons and Angles, the ancestors of the Yankees, came from the cold and marshy regions of the north, where man is little more than an amphibious biped." He assumes, further, "that the Union has served its purposes; that at the North the progress and tendency of opinion was to pure democracy; that the South must so modify its institutions as to remove the people farther from the direct exercise of power; that it was a characteristic of the progress of opinion in the South, that all men see the necessity of more and stronger government; that the people of the South were the most aristocratic people in the world; and, to conclude, that aristocracy is the only safeguard of liberty, and the only power watchful and strong enough to exclude monarchal despotism." I cite these passages for the purpose of showing the repugnance of the author, and the school to which he belongs, to the democratic principle in government.

In an Essay written by J. Quitman Moore of Mississippi, and published in De Bow's Review, in 1861, the author makes the following postulate: "Those pestilent and pernicious dogmas, 'the greatest good to the greatest number,' 'the majority shall rule,' are, in their practical application, the fruitful source of disorders never to be quieted, revolutions the most radical and sanguinary, philosophies the most false, and passions the most wild, destructive, and ungovernable." "In America," says this author, "by reason of the operations of causes wholly extraneous to considerations of government and society, the republican experiment has been favored and prolonged beyond recorded precedent; but, painful as the reflection must be to all such as subscribed to the utopian philosophy, and have an abiding faith in the capacity of man for continuous and enlightened self-rule, it must be confessed that the experiment of the democratic Republic of America has failed."

"The Remedy.—The institution of an hereditary senate and executive is the political form best suited to the genius, and most expressive of the ideas, of the South; but, at the same time, a polity wholly incapable of realization, so long as the individual States retain the attribute of independent sovereignty, and party passions and interests are permitted to stifle the expression of an enlightened and patriotic public sentiment."

"The institution of an hereditary senate and executive the political form best suited to the genius, and most expressive of the ideas of, the South"!!! If this mode of thinking is applied to the slaveholders as a class, the declaration is true beyond a doubt; but, if it is intended to apply to the seven millions non-slaveholding masses, the democratic element in the South, it is not true, even in degree, and mortal man, professing to stand in the image of his maker, never unsealed his lips to utter so foul and detestable a falsehood.

In this programme for a Southern government, we have also an illustration of Southern hypocrisy in relation to the much-vaunted "State-rights" doctrine. It has been used as a pretense, a means to assist in throwing off the national jurisdiction. In the minds of the traitors it meant nothing more. It was merely used as a catchword to inaugurate treason. As soon as revolution was supposed to be accomplished, another and a very different doctrine is immediately put forth. A consolidated government, an hereditary senate and executive, suddenly become the political form "best suited to the genius" of these recent advocates of State rights.

Mr. Stephens, of Georgia, at the time of giving in his adhesion to the Southern Confederacy, had the candor to acknowledge, in part, the hypocrisy of the South as to the reasons for secession. He urged the indispensable necessity of founding a new government, based on the social system of the South, with "Slavery as its corner-stone." Mr. Spratt, of S. C., in his famous letter to Perkins, of Louisiana, reproves the disingenuous accusations against the North made by Southern politicians, stating that no man who deserved the name of statesman in the South would pretend that secession was caused by any aggression of the North upon the rights of the people of the South; that it was still less the result of any act on the part of the United States Government." His argument in favor of taking the government from the "heels of society" and placing it in "the head," is quite as significant of meaning as Mr. Moore's proposition for an hereditary senate and executive.

As incident to a combined monarchal and aristocratic form of government, it is well known that entails and the rights of primogeniture are indispensable. In an article written by George Fitzhugh, of Va., and published in De Bow's Review in 1859, advocating entails and primogeniture, he says—

"Entails of land should include enough to sustain and keep employed at various arts and avocations an almost independent social circle. The landowner's spare profits should enable him to educate well and start in life his younger sons, either as mechanics, artists, or professional men, and, with economy, to lay up small portions for his daughters. To effect these objects, he must have a farming tenantry, with hired laborers under them, or must farm it himself, and employ many laborers. These, with his younger children, and elder ones not in business, and poor and dependent relatives, would form a natural and patriarchal circle, secure from the fluctuations of trade. In all but name, the owner of the entailed estate would be the master, and his family, tenants, laborers, and dependents his servants. It would be an easy way of getting back to predial slavery, without incurring the odium of the name. Give us entails, and we promise you a mild and modified form of domestic slavery. We are no experimenting socialist; we propose nothing new, but only to return to the institutions ordained by God, and tested and approved by human experience."

I might continue these recitals, indicating the intentions of those who inaugurated the rebellion; but, I have not time to proceed with them further on this occasion. These secret motives to overthrow free government in the south, were as carefully concealed from the non-slaveholding masses in the South as they were from the twenty millions in the North. Had they been promulgated as the basis of revolution, the conspiracy would have been crushed by Southern strength alone. The traitors would have been hurled from place and power by the democratic masses, had the secret motives to the treason been understood; but, the masses in the South had been as much deceived by false pretences and the hypocrisy of the leading traitors, as the freemen of the North. The twenty-seven millions, North and South, have been alike deceived, and most of them are laboring under the same delusion to-day.

It was indispensably necessary to the purposes of the rebellion, that false pretences and false motives should be held out. When the rebels entered upon the plot of treason many years ago, political strategy was the great weapon with which to inaugurate it. They had no more scruple on the score of falsehood and deceit than military men have under the usages of war. Whilst they professed to love the Government and the Union, they were hypocritically plotting to overthrow it. They used every art to gain confidence with Northern men, whilst secretly intending to betray it. We have still many men in the North, as well as in the South, who are yet blinded as to the real motives of the traitors, and I have sometimes thought that those most deluded were connected with the administration at Washington, and the generals who are commanding, not to say leading, our armies.

The great mistake that has been made by the administration, and the leading influences that have controlled it, has grown out of the idea that slaveholders as a class, could be conciliated—that some arrangement could be made whereby the South could be restored through their agency. The continuation of that mistake, if persisted in, will lose the whole Union cause. The slaveholding conspirators are haters of democracy. To get rid of democracy and its future sway under the laws of population and subsistence, they risked the institution of slavery; they risked the ravages of war; they risked life, and all that humanity holds most dear; but it must be remembered, that all this risk was incurred, believing that a new order of government, subverting the democratic principle, must be instituted in order to perpetuate and maintain slavery unimpaired.

When we look at the nature of the institution, and the results flowing from it, we can discover the strong pecuniary motive for maintaining it. Aside from the profits of agricultural products, sixty millions pèr year were added to the increase of slave property through the laws of generation. Three per cent, or thereabouts, annually compounded, added to the profits of agriculture, swelled the slaveholders' profits to 10, 12 or 15 per cent. annually. This enabled the slaveholders to monopolize the good lands and the force to cultivate them. In this way the institution was peculiarly calculated to perpetuate wealth in families, and to continuate it in the family descent. But how was this descent of property, and this increase of the future millions upon millions of slaves to be held in bondage? Here were seven millions of non-slaveholders, composing the democratic element of the South. It was an enfrachised, voting power. It was attached to free government, and had drank in the idea of free government the same and as fully as the people of the North. This population in twenty-three to twenty-five years would swell to fourteen millions. Five decades would swell it to twenty-eight millions, whilst the same length of time would swell the slaveholding elements to six millions only. Antagonisms between these democratic and anti-democratic forces were sure to rise up as population became crowded. Under this regime, the antagonistic elements in society, under the laws of population and subsistence, must soon come in conflict.

There was another consideration with slaveholders, and one of most vital energy in impelling them to the project of taking away the power of the masses. The property in slaves was political property. It depended for its duration upon the action of political forces and the policy of the State under the operation of those political forces: hence slaveholders were jealous of the masses. They were anti-democratic, from supposed necessity. They must possess and wield the exclusive political power of the State, and continue to exercise it, for whenever they lost it, and the prestige of its antagonism should come into the ascendency, the downfall of slavery would take its date. This process of reasoning, whether true or false, was the theory of the slaveholding interests in the South. It was the impelling motive, not only for the conspiracy to throw off the national jurisdiction, but to overthrow free government in the South. When these considerations are taken into account, and the motives and purposes of slaveholders analyzed, the fallacy of attempting to conciliate them becomes apparent. Their aim and object is, and from supposed necessity, to overthrow democracy. The effort to do this is backed not only by supposed necessity, in order to preserve slavery unimpaired, but by the whole train of ambitious motives connected with the raising up of an organized and cemented aristocracy.

When we contemplate Southern population, and separate it into classes—to say nothing of the negro—we find seven millions non-slaveholding population, democratic in its sentiments, attached to free government, and in every essential a natural element of national strength in connection with liberalized institutions. When we look at the North, we find twenty millions having the same natural motives. How is it, and why is it, that fifteen hundred thousand men, women, and children, connected in proprietorship in slavery, should have wielded a power and influence that have set the twenty-seven millions at variance, destroyed concert of action, and brought our Government to the deplorable spectacle now witnessed? Is it because, as slaveholders pretend, that "they are our natural masters"? or is it because the twenty-seven millions have been deceived—are now engaged in deceiving each other—and have been frittering away their strength and substance on the most fallacious of all delusions—the belief that the agencies which inaugurated the rebellion can be turned into an agency to restore the Union? If this be the reliance, in my belief the Union is gone.

It has been apparent to my mind, and, as I have often thought, clearly apparent, that an appeal should be made to the democratic element of the South, which as yet has never been spoken to by the Cabinet or Congress at Washington. It is now getting to be known that the political rights and liberty of this population are conspired against. It has long been known that the democracy-haters of Europe were in alliance with the traitors of the South to assist in the prostration of the democratic principle. Why should not the President of the United States proclaim to this democratic element of the South the intent of the traitors to disfranchise the masses, and to erect upon the ruins of their political rights an hereditary aristocracy? Why should not the President say to this population, "The Constitution *as it is* guarantees you free republican government, and, by all the powers in me vested, you shall have it"? Why does he not say to the democracy of the South, "The Constitution *as it is* interdicts the establishment of any order of nobility, and, by the powers in me vested, I declare that it shall *not* be established"? Why does he not command the generals of the army to forego their deluded sympathy in the cause of the traitors, and look to the interests of the Southern masses, whose rights are invaded and trodden down? This folly of attempting to conciliate in the wrong direction, and to fight in the wrong direction, has actually prostrated the public confidence in the administration, in the generalship of the armies, and in our financial power of endurance. This policy must be altered, or the Union is gone; and if the separation is once consummated, the restoration will never transpire.

If men would but reason with accuracy, and determine in their own minds as to what is a democratic element, and therefore an element of national strength—what is anti-democratic, and therefore, an intolerable element of national weakness—our governmental and military forces, as well as the whole people of the North, would at once be brought to act as a unit. The *political moral* of the democratic idea, in connection with arms, must fight this rebellion. If we can succeed in getting the democratic hand, North and South, laid upon this monster rebellion, we shall hear the death-rattle in its throat at once. This is what the traitors are most afraid of. This is what their apprehensions will be most sedulous to guard against. Every art of hypocrisy and false pretence will be put in requisition to prevent it. This is the vulnerable point of attack, and the rebels know it. Negro proclamations may be alarming, but this strikes another and a very different chord of sympathy in the South. It would strike upon the seven millions who have all the natural motives to political affinity with the North—the same educational motives, the same industrial motives, the same social motives, and every other motive connected with the desire to maintain free and liberal government. When we appreciate the full meaning of this conspiracy, and take the traitors at their word in presenting the issue, we shall all know how to act. When the Government and the Generals of our armies rise to the magnitude of the issue as the traitors have tendered it, *they* will know how to act. Treason and civil war were resorted to in order to overthrow free democratic government, because such government was "incompatible with slavery." This is the whole issue, when stripped of the false pretences that have thrown a misguided public opinion around the various incidents of the question. Let us rise to the issue in its true meaning and magnitude. When this is done, the North will become a unit. Let us appeal to the democratic masses in the South on this issue; let the arms of the nation remove the blockade to intelligence, and we shall have the bulk of those masses with us. We must take this course in order to get a strength in the South to assist in restoring the Union; and we must have this strength to hold the South steady after it is restored. We can look in no other direction for competent Southern assistance.

The Slavocracy against Adopted Citizens.

I would here close my remarks, but for an allusion which I wish to make to our adopted citizens, most of whom are in the North. Many illiberal opinions have been expressed towards this population, and more particularly by the slaveholders of the South. Allow me to cite a passage from the writings of the literary pioneer of the Know-Nothing Order. J. Fenton Mercer, of Virginia, who describes himself as a slaveholder, a man of seventy years' experience, and who is known to have held high and responsible offices for many years of his life, was a perfect type and representative man of this order of politicians. In a book written by him, published in 1845, we find the following passage: "Why has not general suffrage destroyed the confederation? This lowest level of political corruption; this universal suffrage; this rule of vagabondism; this rushing into the temple of liberty by the Irish, Dutch and English, with unclean hands, to pollute and deface every thing sacred to the cause of freedom—are sure to defile all, undo all, and dissolve all that is valued in this confederation, when the time shall come for the consummation of the drama."

It is an easy thing, my friends, for men to rail at a class, but it is always more magnanimous to cast about, and ascertain, if we can, whether the class railed at be, or be not, an element of national strength. I have had much experience in dealing with the different elements that compose and sway political organizations. I here declare to you that I have never known an instance, in the maladministration of government, where the iniquity proceeded from the influence of what are termed the "lower orders of society." Those in the humbler walks of life cannot at a single step overleap the intermediate classes, and stand in the high places where mischievous power exerts itself in committing devastation on the public interests. Look at the recent peculations upon the national treasury:—the fault was not with the masses. Look at the recent exhibition of fraud, treason, theft, and hypocrisy connected with the odious administration of Buchanan:—the fault was not with the masses of population, either native or adopted. I could refer you to thousands of instances where men in high places, elected by the honest and well-meaning suffrages of all classes, have betrayed their trust, and engaged in the enactment of laws designed solely for mercenary speculation. Political theft is different from all other kinds of larceny. It exceeds in moral turpitude all others, and is of too high a grade for men in the lower walks of life to be engaged in committing. Political fraud and political peculation, like military glory, seldom get below the captains.

I would now contrast these adopted citizens, and their conduct, with the conduct of these exalted Virginians and their co-revilers in the South, whose writings for years have teemed with ribaldry and revilement against democracy, against our naturalization laws, and against that class of our citizens made partakers of political power under them. These revilers in the South have long been engaged in the plot to overthrow the national jurisdiction and the political rights of the masses. Those who have been reviled are standing by the Government to maintain our free institutions. The examples in contrast should dispel illiberality, as well as the great error in which it was conceived. I admonish my countrymen to indulge in this hateful error of Southern extraction no longer—for, let me assure you that if you persist in this illiberal course, the future historic names of Sigel, and Corcoran, and their hundred and fifty thousand brave companions in arms, will prove, and justly prove, your everlasting rebuke. Calamity, it has often been said, brings out the truth or falsity of theories, inasmuch as it applies the touchstone of truth, which is found in result. I confess to you, my fellow-citizens, that when I see our adopted citizens exposing themselves to the diseases of camp life, the casualties of the battle-field, and standing side by side with our native-born to maintain free democratic government, my admiration and affection towards them are not only confirmed, but intensified. It makes me feel grateful to know that treason, or sympathy with treason, have no place in their hearts. Truly, they are an element of NATIONAL STRENGTH.

LETTERS TO HON. ANDREW JOHNSON.

The following letters to ANDREW JOHNSON of Tennessee, when in Congress last year, will further illustrate the views expressed in the speeches of Col. Hamilton and Lorenzo Sherwood, respecting the real objects of the rebel slaveholders, and indicating the proper antidote for the treason:

NEW YORK, November 25th. 1861

HON. ANDREW JOHNSON (in Senate),
Washington, D. C.

Dear Sir: What are the American armies fighting about, and what the purpose to be gained by the result of arms—are grave questions now being agitated by all classes in Europe. "What are we fighting for?" is a question with many people in the North, who have drank in the impression that the South was composed of nothing but pro-slavery interests.

I will tell you in few words what I am fighting for. I am engaged in this contest, as far as in me lies, in behalf of the non-slaveholding population in the Southern States. You know its character, and you know, at the same time, the disparagement under which it has been placed as an aggregate, ever since its birth; and you also know the helpless, hopelss condition in which it would be placed by the slaveholding power, in case it is permanently separated from its natural political affinity with the North. You know enough of the plans of secession to know its designs upon the mass of free labor South. If you do not, please trace the pages of De Bow's Review for the last ten years, and put what you find cropping out in those pages with what you must have listened to coming from individuals of high standing, and I think you need not be at a loss to discover the ultimate plan of half disfranchising the free labor of the South. It is true, this design has been covered with all but masonic secrecy; but it has, nevertheless, been sufficiently disclosed, and continuously disclosed for the last ten years, to convince me that I am not mistaken.

The slaveholder of the South fears that the voting power of the South may become the governing power. In all my conversations with the intellectual politicians, I have observed this jealousy, this fear; and what has troubled the pro-slavery spirit most of all things, has been the contemplated probability of an affinity between the free labor North and South. When that transpires, it will prove the destruction of the pro-slavery prestige, even in the South; and we shall hear no more of plans to break up the Government, or to dismember the Union.

I have grown wearied and disgusted with the mawkish sensibility over the negro, when there is so much higher and more available ground to take in favor of the white man. Six and one-half or seven millions of white men, —their half-disparaged condition; their fitness to be free men, and their right to be disenthralled from the prejudice which the pro-slavery spirit in politics has thrust upon them—afford to my mind a just basis for Governmental consideration in the prosecution of this war.

I wish to say plainly, Sir, my sympathies are enlisted in the great cause of *white humanity in its shirt-sleeves*—of that twenty seven millions of American free citizens who are bound to the eternal business of subsistence through their own industry. Their lot is to toil—to toil on from generation to generation; and a pretty business it is for less than one hundred thousand rebel slaveholders to set these toiling millions to cutting one another's throats!

What right, have we of the North to abandon our white non-slaveholding brethren of the South to the hopeless tyranny of an exclusive pro-slavery policy? What right has Congress to forbear the bold declaration in favor of this population, and to pledge all the adhering elements of the Government to protect it—to shelter it under the national ensign—yea, if need be, to so far humble and subordinate the pro-slavery spirit as to give encouragement in the right direction to the masses of the Southern white population?

It would be useless to say "this non-slaveholding population cannot be reached." It can be reached, and can be enlisted on the side of its own protection. Let Congress and all the governmental powers declare their solicitude for it, and determination to protect it; and let us of the North re-echo the sentiment, and hail it as a brotherhood in political destiny and political right. Arms will remove the blockade to intelligence. We shall have the mass of this population with us if we take the bold and strong means to invite it.

It strikes me that you are the man to bring out this subject through a congressional declaration. Your sympathies are known to be with the masses of the laboring white men South. You are known and marked in every part of the Union as their friend. You have the courage to do just what your conscience tells you is best. Congresses and conventions have been truckling to rebel slaveholders and endeavoring to salve over their antipathies to the Union. No effort has made them better. Nothing can make them worse. Suppose the effort should now be made in the direction where the process of reasoning would naturally carry it. Nothing can be lost by making the attempt. A bold declaration would strike more terror into the minds of rebel slaveholders, than half a dozen Port Royal cannonades—terrific as that affair appeared. It would be worthy an American Congress and command the approval of the world. The question, "What are we fighting for," would no longer be asked.

Very truly yours, &c.,

LORENZO SHERWOOD.

NEW YORK, *November* 28, 1861.

HON. ANDREW JOHNSON (in Senate),
Washington, D. C.

Dear Sir:

What is practicable and what is *not* practicable, by way of raising up a Southern Union party, or co-operating strength, is now the question. That there should be a congressional declaration of something else than worn-out generalities, I have no doubt. That there should be something said that is sufficiently specific to strike upon some chord of natural sympathy, appears more and more to me to be necessary.

The suggestions I forwarded to you have gained upon my mind since I wrote you, and the policy of an appeal to the free labor South, and the separation of the Southern population into classes, so as to throw the responsibility of the rebellion upon the small numerical class that inaugurated it, is more apparent to my mind than when I last wrote you.

I think we have much to gain by Southern indiscretion. The slip I send you is indicative of the developing design of secession, and is corroborative of the motive I alluded to in the suggested resolutions.

The moral force of the Southern programme must be struck at its vulnerable point. What is that vulnerable point? My long residence in the extreme South convinces me that the intended disfranchisement of the Southern masses is the most prominent cause of Southern discontent; and that the exemplification of this intent by a congressional declaration would tend to establish a more effective hold upon the Union sentiment South, than any thing else that could be put forth.

I am aware that nearly every Union man, South, who has been accustomed to play the Southern political game in politics, is stereotyped in the idea that any thing that tends directly or remotely to the policy of emancipation should be avoided. They seem to forget the political necessity of making the declaration to the effect, that *protection and allegiance must go together;* that this is a political, social, national, and above all, in the midst of the effusion of blood, an imperious and unavoidable war necessity. We shall come to this, and the sooner the declaration is made, in connection with other considerations, in my humble opinion the better.

In the midst of tribulation, under democratic government, every sensitive man of impulse persuades himself into the belief that he is a competent adviser. We shall have a thousand and one distractions as to the declared motives which exist for the prosecution of the war. They are already being put forth in different sections, and the Government at Washington is as little understood in its views of policy as in its unpublished military designs. I think it time, in order to avoid public distraction in the North, and to show to the world that there is such a thing as definite motive in Government policy, founded on some tangible principle, to make an authoritative congressional declaration of some kind; and the more pointed it is, if founded on just principle, the better. I doubt whether you could find an abolitionist *per se* who would strike the right point. I also doubt whether any politician from the Gulf States, however strong in his Union sentiments, would dare venture upon any definite declaration that would be specific. You will excuse my suggestions; they are made under the belief that something effective must be done in connection with arms to raise up a Southern strength to our side. If we cannot do it, the Union is gone. I hope it may never be said of us, that we have lost our strength and the force of the Union cause through timidity.

Are we not brought by the determined spirit of rebellion to deal with all its opposing elements affirmatively? Has not all forbearance been construed into timidity? It has seemed to me that the disposition to forego as long as possible any resort to force by the national Government has been an ill-devised humanity, that has reresulted merely in preparation for a more extensive effusion of blood. If anything is yet to be gained by paltering to the influences that have inaugurated this treason against the common population and common interest of the country, I cannot see it. Perhaps those better skilled in political philosophy may be able to do so. I fear, however, that those who have so long failed to appreciate the nature, strength, and motives of this rebellion will be slow—quite too slow—in the enunciation of views or principles in connection with the plan of raising up a Southern party, and of strengthening the North by keeping it a unit.

Very truly, &c.,

LORENZO SHERWOOD.

(POSTSCRIPT TO THE SECOND EDITION.)

From the New York Tribune, Oct. 21.

The "Origin and Objects of the Slaveholders' Conspiracy against Democratic Principles, as well as against the National Union," illustrated in the Speeches of Andrew Jackson Hamilton, of Texas, the statements of Lorenzo Sherwood, late of Texas; the letter of Muscoe R. H. Garnett, late Democratic Member of Congress from Virginia, to William H. Trescott, of South Carolina, showing the antagonism of Democracy and Free Labor to Slavery and its Rebellion; the Letter of the Democratic League of our City to John Bright, &c., has just been compiled for that League by Henry O'Rielly, and is now printed in a neat pamphlet, which can be had at our office. If there is a sincere and loyal Democrat in this State, who now thinks of voting for Seymour & Co., we are confident that a careful reading of this pamphlet would dissuade him from so doing. Please look into it, and judge if you ought not to aid in circulating it.

www.ingramcontent.com/pod-product-compliance
Lightning Source LLC
LaVergne TN
LVHW011141110826
845150LV00008B/2450

* 9 7 8 1 4 1 8 1 9 2 9 7 6 *